HISTORY in a HURRY

Aztecs

written and drawn by
JOHN FARMAN

MACMILLAN
CHILDREN'S BOOKS

First published 1998 by Macmillan Children's Books
a division of Macmillan Publishers Limited
25 Eccleston Place, London SW1W 9NF
and Basingstoke

Associated companies throughout the world

ISBN 0 330 35247 4

Text and illustrations copyright © John Farman 1998

The right of John Farman to be identified as the
author of this work has been asserted by him in accordance with the
Copyright, Designs and Patents Act 1988.

All rights reserved. No reproduction, copy or transmission
of this publication may be made without written permission.
No paragraph of this publication may be reproduced, copied or
transmitted except with written permission or in accordance with
the provisions of the Copyright Act 1956 (as amended). Any
person who does any unauthorized act in relation to
this publication may be liable to criminal prosecution
and civil claims for damages.

1 3 5 7 9 8 6 4 2

A CIP catalogue record for this book is available from
the British Library.

Printed and bound in Great Britain
by Mackays of Chatham plc, Kent

CONTENTS

	Off we go!	4
1	The Historical Bit	6
2	Tenochtitlan (pronounced Ten-Knock-Tit-Lan)	10
3	Aztecs Tuck In – Which Way To Grow?	14
4	At Home with the Aztecs	20
5	How to Spot an Aztec in the Street	24
6	Aztec-lings – Kids for Sale	31
7	Human Sacrifice – or... Meet 'Em, Join 'Em, Beat 'Em, Eat 'Em	38
8	What a very odd lot they were – Aztec Gods	46
9	Those Dratted Spanish! or... All Good Things Come to an End	53
10	New Spain	60
	Time's Up	64

💨 *OFF WE GO!*

If, like me (or like I was before I wrote this book), you hardly know your Aztecs from your Incas, you might find my little book of some use. I don't know about you, but I'd always thought that the Aztec civilization existed way back in antiquity, around the time of the Ancient Egyptians and Co, and was more than somewhat surprised to find out that they only ran out of steam (with a little help from the Spanish) in 1521 – around the time of our Henry VIII. The whole caboodle only lasted 200 years (a mere drip in a bucket, history-wise).

It's odd to think that while over in Europe we were well into the Renaissance (art, culture and all that), in Aztec-land they were sacrificing each other on a regular basis.

It's even odder to think that these same Aztecs built beautiful cities of such quality that modern architects could still learn a thing or two from them.

Oddest of all, our late William Shakespeare was born only thirty years after the demise of their civilization and while he wrote using words of such astounding sophistication, their literature consisted only of simple stories with weeny pictures (they were probably too busy eating each other to bother with niceties like communication).

Ah well, that's history for you.

Oh, by the way, if you notice a few annoying scribbles by someone called 'Ed' in this book, I'm really sorry, but it's Susie, my picky editor* – we didn't have time to change them before the book got printed.

AVERAGE AZTECS

*Just doing my job! Ed

Chapter 1

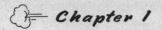 **THE HISTORICAL BIT**

Where From?
The Aztecs had originally descended from the tribes of hunter-gatherers from Asia, hunting roots and berries and gathering animals,* who, 30,000 years earlier, had stumbled across to the Americas over the land bridge we now call the Bering Straits. They settled on that thinnish strip between the north bit and the south bit of America.

By AD1000, there were lots of different peoples occupying this vast land (now Mexico – check it out on an atlas, I hate drawing maps) mostly with names ending in 'tec', but it was a tribe called the Tenochcas (pronounced Ten-Knock-Ass) or Mexicas (Mec-Sick-Ass) who by 1200 had become the Aztecs (Az-Tecs). Being the last to turn up, they had to wander around for donkey's years trying to find somewhere to settle down.

Home at Last
Eventually they set up home on a deserted swampy island called Aztlan in the middle of Lake Texcoco (Az + Tex; geddit?) – not because they wanted to, but because the other

---

*Shouldn't that be the other way round? Ed

tribes were extremely beastly to them and wouldn't let them live anywhere else. Needless to say, after all that wandering around they were ever so poor when they started building their first reed-hut village in 1325, but in no time at all they'd spread onto all the other littler islands and knocked up a magnificent city and headquarters called Tenochtitlan (the Place of the Cactus) where Mexico City is now.

Aztecs Fight Back
As they grew bigger and stronger the Aztecs started being extremely horrid back to all those tribes that had given them a hard time in the first place. They must have surprised even themselves at how good they were at foe-fighting, and the fearsome Aztec armies quickly spread across the surrounding countryside punishing all the other tribes that got in their way. Soon they occupied most of Mexico, either building or conquering (so much quicker, I find) 500 cities of all shapes and sizes. The surrounding lands were linked to Tenochtitlan by a series of man-made causeways.

These conquests really revved up under their best leader Montezuma I (1440–69) who sent huge armies to wipe out their last big enemy, the Mixtecs (presumably an assortment of different 'tecs') who lived on the lands over to the east. All was going extremely well until 1519, when someone spotted what looked to be a horde of white visitors in boats as big as

mountains arriving at the coast (the Aztecs were always big on exaggeration). Two years later the whole civilization was wiped out (see Chapter 9). That's tourism for you.

Pictures not Words
We know loads and loads about the Aztecs because, as I mentioned before, they left loads and loads of wonderful picture books called *codices* (actually they *had* to be picture

books because they never got the hang of writing – joined-up or otherwise). From these books, and from the ruins they left behind, we learn that despite human sacrifice, child-eating and mass slavery, it was, in fact, an empire of great invention and beauty. Let's take a closer look.

Chapter 2

TENOCHTITLAN
(pronounced
Ten-Knock-Tit-Lan)

When the Spanish reached the Valley of Mexico in 1519 they must have been fairly surprised to find dozens of little towns and villages hugging the shores of Lake Texcoco. But on the large island in the middle of the lake was a sight that knocked them into the middle of next week. A mighty, gleaming city of 200,000 people which looked like it shot straight out of the water. They had never seen anything like it before.

As Tenochtitlan had ended up much larger than the island they'd started building it on, thousands of stakes had had to be driven into the surrounding lake (only 3 to 4 metres deep) to provide a sound base for the foundations.* Three massive causeways, wide enough for ten wide soldiers, led to the city, with wooden drawbridges that could be pulled away if they were being attacked. They even had aqueducts bringing fresh water to supply the fountains and reservoirs (and presumably the population).

The city was laid out in a surprisingly modern-style grid, a bit like New York, divided by canals which, just like Venice, acted as main roads (albeit rather damp ones). The city was vast and immaculate, the streets (the ones which

---

*Doesn't sound very sound to me. Ed

weren't canals) being swept and sprinkled with water every day. They even had public lavs (I'd have used the canal).

> ### Useless Fact No. 44
> As there were no proper farm animals (there being no proper farms), there would have been a severe shortage of manure or fertilizer for their crops. Three guesses where they collected sufficient supplies from?*

Over to the east was a huge dyke, fifteen kilometres long, which had been dug to regulate the level of the lake using sluice gates. It also prevented the salt water mucking up their gardens.

There were four main sectors of the city, each one containing a market area, with its own temples and schools. The markets sold everything from food, clothing, skins, weapons, canoes and herbs to electric lawnmowers.

In the Temple Precinct of the Teopan quarter were the fabbest structures of all, dedicated to their best gods. Nearby stood a charming little feature, a wall built from the skulls of their dead enemies. The Great Temple with the twin shrines of top gods Tlaloc (pronounced Tlay-Lock) and Huitzilopochtli (I give in from now on), was astounding, sharing a single 30 metre high pyramid, on top of which they did a lot of their sacrificing (more about this later!). Near to this temple was another dedicated to Quetzalcoatl which had a door shaped like a terrible mouth (the Jaws of Hell)

*That's disgusting. Ed
Don't blame me. JF

beside which were the chopping blocks and pots filled with water ready for the butchering and cooking of those unfortunate enough to be providing lunch that day. The inside walls were decorated with carved statues smothered in gold and encrusted with the most precious of jewels, as were all the many temples, but unfortunately they were also splashed with human blood and as a result smelt worse than any slaughter-house.

Gob-Smacked
You can imagine the Spanish visitors' jaws dropping when they stumbled on all of this, especially the palace of Axayacatl (you try) which was so huge it could accommodate the Spaniards' entire army.

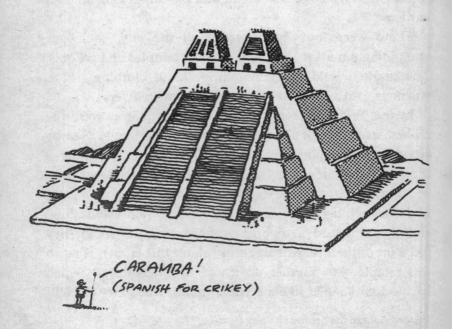

CARAMBA!
(SPANISH FOR CRIKEY)

But that was nothing compared to Montezuma's palace, which was like a small town in itself. There were halls so big that they could hold three thousand people, all decorated with beautiful frescoes, silver and gold plaques and precious stones.* Everywhere the gobsmacked Spaniards looked were beautiful villas and gardens with bathing pools cut out of the rock. There were zoos and aviaries full of fierce beasts of prey and exotic, unseen-before tropical birds. It was like paradise – well, to look at, anyway . . .

*Do you mean the halls or the people? Ed
The people, silly. JF

Chapter 3

AZTECS TUCK IN – WHICH WAY TO GROW?

One of the many drawbacks of being unpopular with practically everyone was that the very early Aztecs had to do everything for themselves (no slaves involved yet). The biggest problem was food, and the second biggest problem was how to grow it.* Being squeezed onto a series of tiny islands meant there was a shortage of earth to plant things in. And it was no good asking their nasty neighbours on the mainland if they could borrow some of theirs, as they were known to be exceedingly stroppy, rather unhelpful and quite possessive when it came to land.

An Agricultural Puzzle

So here you are, living in the middle of a tiny lake in the middle of Mexico. You have as much fertile mud (from the bottom of the lake) as you could ever want; you have limitless bucketfuls of water (from the top of the lake); you have more reeds than you know what to do with, and, best of all, loads of bright, hot sunshine; but – and here's the big BUT – you have no land to grow things in. What would *you* do if *you* were an Aztec (or even if you weren't)?

*Same thing, surely. Ed

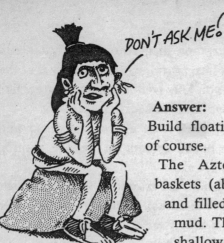

DON'T ASK ME!

Answer:
Build floating gardens (*chinampas*), of course.

The Aztecs wove trillions of baskets (about 2.5 metres square) and filled them with lake-bottom mud. These they fastened in the shallow waters all around the islands, planted willows round them for protection, chucked in seeds and, hey presto, had all the extra land (and, therefore, all the extra grub) they needed.

Clever, eh?

What to Grow?

It stands to reason that living on islands surrounded by water meant that there would have been a lot of fish to eat. So what goes nicely with fish, apart from chips and mushy peas (which hadn't been invented)?

Sweetcorn (or maize, to call it by its proper name) was the answer.

Useless Fact No. 48
Just to show how important maize was to the Aztecs, one of their top gods, Quetzalcoatl, always walked around with five corn-on-the-cobs strapped to his bottom, presumably in order never to be caught short (or, more likely, because he was totally round the bend).

Amaizing

Maize quickly became their staple diet. You could grind it, boil it, bake it, slice it, make it into porridge (*atole*), throw it at the mother-in-law – anything you jolly well liked; and it grew like crazy in the hot, damp conditions of Mexico.

When fed up with fish, there were millions of ducks and their various beaky chums bobbing about on the lake, waiting to be added to the menu.

Later, when they moved onto the mainland with their bows and arrows (the Aztecs, not the ducks), there were rabbits, deer and peccaries (wild pigs) if they were still a little peckarish*. They even caught wild dogs with nets and ate them too.

Best and biggest of all were the llamas but, as you can imagine, the downside of eating them was that it tended to impair their use as beasts of burden.

*That joke needs locking up. Ed

Oh, I almost forgot, the other great culinary delight of a meatular nature was each-other. The Aztecs were big on cannibalism (see Barbecue Recipes later).

More Beans
The other mainstay of their diet was beans – loads and loads of beans. Nutritionists would say this was perfect for the balanced diet, but they didn't have to share confined spaces with 'em.

Tamales
I hope you haven't eaten recently. If you have, try to make sure you read this near a bucket.

The poorer Aztecs used to make these sort of maize envelopes called *tamales* which they stuffed with a variety of frogs, newts, slugs, snails (and puppy dogs' tails?), insect eggs, ants, grasshoppers (boiled) and, hold on to your stomach, those disgusting little red worms that you often find living squirmily in the mud at the bottom of lakes.

Yum, yum! But I suppose you might prefer this to eating your mates?

Useless Fact No. 50
Have you ever seen those poncy midget dogs called Chihuahuas, much favoured by rich old ladies? The Aztecs used to breed their little hairless, barkless ancestors at home and, when fed up with them as pets (not difficult), served them up for Sunday lunch. These little canine baldies were described by one historian as 'sad faced and uncomplaining even when beaten'* (sounds like John Major). I think the fact that they were unable to bark might have had something to do with that.

*Shouldn't that be eaten? Ed
I'll do the jokes, thank you. JF

Hot Chocolate

Rich Aztecs went in for feasts at the drop of a hat (or a headdress). They got hold of marvellous food: pineapples and other exotic fruits from distant lands; crabs, oysters and turtles from the coast; and, for afters, a sort of drinking chocolate – *chocolatl* (honestly) – made from the cacao nut and whipped up into a cold frothy drink and flavoured with spices (not bad, eh?).

Pulque

The poor people usually drank water, but on festival days were allowed *pulque* (sounds like puke*), a rather yukky beverage made from the fermented sap of the cactus. Unfortunately, if they had a little too much of it, and got a bit – how should we say – tipsy, they could expect to be put to death which, you must admit, would make you think twice. Makes our alcohol laws seem a bit puny! On *very* special days, however, the peasants were given a licence to drink *and* to get drunk, which they did . . . and did.

Getting the Drugs Out

Strangely enough the Aztecs weren't nearly as uptight about drugs as they were about booze. It was common at festivals to get totally stoned on *peyotl* (from cactus buds) which is now known as the dreaded mescalin, and *teonanacatl*, a bitter black mushroom which made you go temporarily round the bend. It could send you into instant hysterical laughter, have you hanging from the nearest cactus or, even worse, chucking yourself off a cliff (sounds like my home-made beer).

* Must you? Ed

Time for a Puff

You can sort of blame Aztecs for tobacco, as it was first grown in the New World (the Americas) and Mexico. The Aztecs mixed it with flowers and all sorts of sweet-scented substances and then smoked it in long reed pipes.

Meal Times

Most Aztecs would have a nice bowl of *atole* (maize porridge) for breakfast and then wait for their main meal at lunchtime or whenever they stopped work. They usually ate maize tortillas (as found in all good Mexican restaurants) filled with hot, spiced-up vegetables. They then took a little kip before going back to work. Lastly, they'd have another bowl of porridge at bedtime, which was usually, having no telly, when the sun went down. With all that maize, I'd have eaten anybody for a bit of protein.

YOU LOOK GOOD ENOUGH TO EAT, DEAR

Chapter 4

AT HOME WITH THE AZTECS

Living Rough

Most of the poorer people's houses were made out of wattle and daub (sounds like a Welsh folk group) with thatched reed roofs. 'Wattle' is the term for sticks woven together and 'daub' is basically plain ordinary mud (daubed on the wattle). Some of the more industrious peasants got into brick making-and-baking, which was dead easy in the blistering sun.

By law, the Aztec poor were not allowed to have an upper floor (see Stupid Bureaucracy in Ancient Times) but they could paint their huts as brightly as they liked – and boy did

they like bright. Most of these 'houses', for want of a better word, had two rooms – one for eating and sitting about in and the other for sleeping and... er... waking up in. The family's more valuable possessions, of which there were few, were kept in wooden chests while all the other stuff, like digging sticks (no spades yet), hunting and fishing tackle, various pots and pans, the odd simple loom or the grinding stone for maize would be lying about in various corners of the room. They had no water, no windows, no doors* and practically no furniture. The only light came from torches made from pine shavings.

Useless Fact No. 52
As the Aztecs hadn't invented doors, the risk of theft was pretty obvious. However, penalties for stealing were so heavy (like heart removal) that there tended to be little crime.

At the centre of every living room would be an open hearth or 'comal', composed of three stones set in a triangle supporting a clay disc for Mrs Aztec to bake the tortillas on. Because the stones were reckoned to hold all the secrets of the fire god, they were deemed sacred, so anyone who stepped on them was in instant big trouble (along with badly burnt feet).

*How did they get in and out then? Ed
Through the gap where the door should have gone, of course. JF

Every household contained little statues of their gods made of wood, stone or clay, and a talking parrot or songbird hanging in a little cage*. Having no chimney meant that the hut would often be filled with acrid smoke from the wood-burning cooking fire, which was sometimes contained in a clay pot to stop the roof catching fire.

These homes were often in little compounds opening up on a shared courtyard. Each extended family would usually live together, so you'd have the old grandparents in one bit, their married kids in another and adult grandchildren in another.

Anyone for a Sauna?
Many of these Aztec dwellings had an outside steam room, which I find a bit flash when you consider that they hadn't even got a lav. This would be shaped like an igloo and the walls would be heated by an outside furnace till they were red hot. Your average grubby Aztec would then chuck water on the walls, hang around in the steam for a while and then rub himself down with twigs and grass (I'd still want a bath after that).

Stilts or Flats?
Most of the farmers lived on and around the floating gardens that surrounded the little marshy islands (that surrounded

---

*Shouldn't that be 'in a little hanging cage'? Ed

Tenochtitlan). They lived in reed huts on stilts or on huge platforms sometimes up to 300 feet in length.

The poorer Tenochtitlaners (the ones who actually made their home in the city) tended to live in the forerunners of flats, with spacious floor areas occupied by large groups of workers rather than individual families. These mostly opened onto the streets or canals and many had little floating *chinampa* allotments nearby to grow their own vegetables.

Posh Pads

The richer nobles had housing well sussed. They lounged around in large, square, mud-brick villas with shady courtyards in the middle (or is that middles?). They'd usually have a dining room, a bedroom with canopied reed beds, a reception room, a kitchen, a servants' apartment and, rather ominously, a punishment room. As no one had bothered to invent locks to put on doors that you now know didn't exist, rich people's entrances were covered with heavy decorated curtains with little tinkly bells sewn into them, to warn the occupants against intruders or when their mates were arriving. As I said in the chapter on food, their pet dogs were no use as guards as a) they couldn't bark and b) they usually ended up being eaten. As for furniture, the 'Rich-tecs' had strange, high-backed legless chairs (*icpalli*), low tables and braziers for burning wood, and there'd usually be lots of elaborate and colourful wall-hangings and rugs. These houses were most-times flat topped and often planted with lovely roof gardens.

Had enough of this?* Let's get on to something more interesting.

*Yes. Ed

Chapter 5

HOW TO SPOT AN AZTEC IN THE STREET

Most Aztecs looked pretty much the same without their clothes on. They were short, dark-skinned and had black, shiny, dead straight hair cut in a rather trendy 'page-boy' style.

Aztec Lads
Men, especially warriors, would often have a silly pony-tail (as are all pony-tails) on the very top of their heads. Your average Aztec would wear a nifty little loincloth with a decorated flap front and back, presumably to cover his rude bits. Over all this he'd throw a cloak or cape held by a knot at the shoulder.

Aztec Babes
The girls wore rather groovy wrap-round fringed skirts held up by a belt, and a sort of tasselled poncho with a hole to put their heads through. All a bit hippyish, but sort of forgivable if you're the first to do it. It generally worked out that the

smarter an Aztec's position in society, the more fancy his clothes turned out to be (nothing's changed there then). Rich people used to wear the most magnificent fabrics, fab jewellery and rather nice hats.

At the Beauty Parlour

Women dabbed their faces with a kind of yellow powder, darkened their feet and hands with burnt copal (resin) and dye (thought to look sexy) and traced intricate little patterns on their necks and hands when going out somewhere special (like a Mexican restaurant). Best of all, they'd use fab little pottery stamps to print brightly coloured patterns on their faces – like pretend tattoos (boys and men had proper ones). They also painted stuff on their intimate parts – but that was only for the eyes of 'special' friends (if you know what I mean). Their lustrous hair was always washed in indigo (blue dye) to give it that 'extra, deeper glow' that the ad men tell us we love so much.

If a girl was to dye her teeth red she was regarded as a bit vulgar (and a bit barmy, I'd have thought). Consequently, it became the best way of recognizing fallen women (apart from untidy hair, walking around with all their bits showing and, rather surprisingly, the constant munching of – wait for it – mushrooms*).

* You're making this up. Ed
No: it's from the Florentine Codex, one of their most important manuscripts, in which it also says that they chewed gum. So there! JF

Useless and Rather Rude Fact No. 53

Ladies of ill repute (the oldest profession in the world) often used to trick their clients into drinking a charming little beverage called *macacoatl* (try asking for that down the 'offie'). This was brewed by stewing a rather nasty sort of smallish snake and supposed to make the drinker extremely amorous (ten times a night amorous). The downside was that following this particular night, he would promptly die looking 'well dried up, with little old eyes, nasal mucus hanging, trembling of neck and his flesh hanging in wrinkles'. Maybe I'll stick to lager.

Feathers for All

One of the great by-products of eating lots of exotic birds is that you are likely to have quite a few exotic feathers left over. Aztecs liked their feathers and involved them in every aspect of their 'Sunday best' and 'going to war' wear. You can always recognize a good Aztec by his or her magnificent head-dress. Feathers were also traded throughout the world, as most people had never seen anything quite so striking. The plumage of the red arrara, the blue and scarlet feathers of the scarlet macaw, the magnificent gold and black troupial were highly prized, but most valuable of all were the long curved tail feathers of the quetzal, a very rare bird from the

rain forests noted for its shyness. (Blimey, I'd be shy if I thought that everyone was trying to pull the feathers out of my bum.)

Gold for All

The Aztecs 'imported' (i.e. nicked) tons of precious metals. One of the best things about having lots of gold around the place (until those dratted Spaniards stole it all) was that they didn't really have to look around for much else to make jewellery out of. Aztec craftsmen were the best in the world and people still imitate their stuff today.

They were also into body piercing (how trendy) in a big way – particularly their noses. Both men and women would wear heavy, solid gold nose furniture, intricately worked pendants and gold, jade and turquoise feathered earrings, anklets and bracelets.

Useless Fact No. 54
The Spanish weren't daft. Cruel, yes – but not daft. In order to get as much gold as possible, they told the Aztecs that they suffered from a nasty disease that only gold could cure (gosh, I think we all suffer from that!).

War Wear

The Aztecs cracked psychological warfare big-time. There's no doubt in my mind that by going to battle in outfits as ridiculous as theirs, the enemy could be made helpless by laughter.

Here are a few little numbers they paraded in front of the enemy, no doubt to keep them amused and somewhat distracted.

🔺 First we have Moctezoma in a skintight jumpsuit in olive-hued, arrow-resistant cotton quilting. It is finished with a huge white bow over the private parts and a helmet shaped like a parrot's head with our model's own head peaking out of its beak. His shoes are cheeky little peep-toe sandals tied with red ribbons. Just the thing for that impromptu little battle when you simply can't think what to wear.

🔺 Skintight again. This time we have Xiutihtli smothered in eagle feathers and with a matching eagle's head helmet. Covering this fashion-warrior's feet are huge bird-foot shoes complete with gold talons. The whole ensemble is finished with a pretty blue bow and a plume of red feathers on the very top of the helmet. Available at all Tenochtitlan stores at a price everyone can afford.

Finally we see young Cihuacotl wearing this season's ocelot skin catsuit with a blue bow covering his essentials and blue feathers coming out of his cat-head helmet. A wonderful addition to anyone's battle wardrobe.

When actually parading on (or near) the battlefield each one carried a plumed spear and an attractive and eye-catching tooled leather shield covered in an assortment of coloured feathers. Blimey, if I saw that lot running towards me I'd practically die laughing. To be fair,* the proper soldiers (the ones that did most of the fighting and getting killed) simply went to battle in a loincloth and bow (but this time for arrows).

Useless Fact No. 60
Aztec soldiers weren't paid, but anyone who captured four or more enemies was promoted to a nobleman. That's incentive for you! If they were lucky enough to be killed they went to a special heaven near the sun (Butlin's?).

*Fair? That makes a change. Ed

Chapter 6

AZTEC-LINGS – KIDS FOR SALE

Being born into an Aztec household carried a certain amount of risk. If you arrived on any one of a few special dates you could be one of those chosen to be sacrificed (to death) to Tlaloc, the rain god, which, it has to be said, is not the best start in life. Somewhat disappointing for the mums and dads, admittedly, but it wasn't all bad news since the priests usually paid them good money for their nippers (so that's all right then). I wonder how much money *your* parents would have taken for you?

The children to be sacrificed were kept in special kindergartens (see Not Very Cheerful Aztec Places) in the weeks, months or even years leading up to their big day. The poor little mites would then be dressed in sumptuous robes, paraded in front of the thronging masses, and then, with no further ado, have their dear little throats cut in front of a large crowd. The floods of tears that this caused amongst the audience (not to mention the odd parent or two) was supposed to encourage rain.

Maybe we should suggest this to the government. We're always running short of water.

Right Height?

Another neat way of choosing who to sacrifice was to match suitable nippers with the current height of the maize crop, thus encouraging growth (beats fertilizer I suppose*). So, when the young plants were just a span (a hand's width), they'd pick tiny babies.

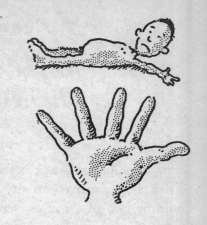

Later, when the maize reached knee height, they'd go for five to seven year old slaves (remember the Aztecs were very small). I suppose when it reached full height they'd sacrifice a few adults – just for good measure.

Short and Useless Fact No. 66
Oddly enough, the tiny babies they picked were always from the families of noblemen. Typical, rich kids get all the best jobs.

Most children, however, were highly prized and, after a birth, the Aztecs would have huge drunken knees-ups that would go on for days.

*And you're very sick – I suppose. Ed

The littl'uns would be expected to learn the skills of their parents: girls – cooking, spinning, cleaning, washing, etc, and boys – their dad's profession, plus, of course, warrioring.

Girl Children
A baby girl would be shown a tiny little spindle, a work basket and a broom in order to get her future role into her head as early as possible. Weirder still, her umbilical cord (detached) would be buried at home in order that she (or it) would refrain from wandering too far. Girls would be given names representing something gentle or pretty, like Quiauhxochitl (Rain Flower), Miahuaxiuitl (Turquoise Maize Flower) or Tziquetzalpoztectzin (the Quetzal Bird). All very well, but it must have taken for ever calling them in for their tea.

Boy Children
A baby boy would be given a miniature warrior's kit or tiny versions of the tools of his dad's trade. As for names, as well as his short pet name of, say, Pete, Ted or Jack, he'd be given much more flashy other names like Angry Turkey, Fire Coyote, Bee in the Reeds, Speaking Eagle or Darren.*

*I don't think so. Ed

Useless Fact No. 70

Aztec discipline was dead strict. Children who were naughty were often beaten, pricked with sharp thorns, tied up and thrown into deep, sloppy mud or, if very bad, held naked over a fire of burning chillies (that's not just hot, but very hot). I think this would've had more effect than being sent to their rooms or not being allowed to watch telly for a couple of hours.

School for Girls

...for the poor

As in most primitive societies girls seldom went to school. In many ways the girl children of the poor had it easier than those of the rich nobles. Even so, most hardly ever left the house until their wedding day (fancy that, girls?) and were expected to work on their handicrafts from dawn to dusk.

... for the nobles
But these were the lucky ones. Those from noble birth were sent away during their early teens to be locked up in the hyper-strict priest schools (*calmecac*) to be taught embroidery. This wasn't done so much to improve their sewing skills but to protect them from the evils of boys (spoilsports!). They usually left at around 15 when the first offers of marriage started coming in.

... for the rulers
A ruler's daughter had an even rougher deal. She had to spend all her time with the old women. She could only go into the gardens with guards, never lift her eyes from the ground and, would you believe it, never look behind her – for fear of severe punishment (and you think *your* parents are strict?). To make matters worse, she was expected to keep absolutely silent, and men weren't even allowed to speak to her.

But in some respects Aztec society was quite sophisticated: there was free education for all children who wanted it (as if!).

Telpochcalli (or House of Youth)
This was the school for the sons of tradesmen and peasants and their attitude was one that ran all the way through Aztec society. The Telpochcalli's sole purpose had nothing to do with expanding the kids' general knowledge, but everything

to do with making them into good, tame citizens. After all, they thought, what's the point of knowing skills if you're never going to use them (sounds reasonable to me!). Taking that to its logical conclusion, why even teach someone to think for himself if there's always going to be some smart-arsed official to do it for him? Still, I suppose it taught the youngsters of the lowly to know their place (and quite right too!).

Calmecac for Boys
These were attached to the temples, and were for all those lucky little chaps that would one day be in charge: priests, military leaders, judges and top civil servants. Guess what, they were the children of . . . those that were in charge, of course.

These were very different to the Telpochcalli schools (see above). For a start, they taught all the major subjects (except computer studies) that the others didn't, and the boys were kept imprisoned behind high walls. These schools worked on the somewhat dodgy principle that if you are going to lead, you must know how to obey, and so saying, the regime was staggeringly strict.

Useless Fact No. 73

One of the only times that the boys got to go out was when sent to a deserted mountain top for an all-night praying session, offering incense and sacrificing blood which they'd collect by pricking themselves in their ears and legs with cactus spines (golly, I can think of things I'd rather do on my night off*).

*I bet you can. Ed

Chapter 7

HUMAN SACRIFICE
or ...
MEET 'EM,
JOIN 'EM
BEAT 'EM,
EAT 'EM

Now sit down and swallow hard – this chapter's certainly not for the squeamish. As I said somewhere else, the Aztecs didn't worship their gods to become better Aztecs (as *we're* all supposed to do) but simply to try to win their favour just in case, in some godly temper tantrum or other, they brought death and destruction on Aztec society. Obviously, the best way of keeping those old gods quiet was to sacrifice the very thing that made the Aztecs themselves tick – the heart and blood of humans (or, oddly enough, the occasional quail). But dying wasn't the end of it. When dead people left this earth, their poor souls had to endure a whole load of trials, one of which was the 'Wind of Hell', which must have been quite a breeze as it was able to strip the flesh off their bones.*
On the plus side, most folk went to their death happy (or so they said) in the knowledge that they were going to a 'better place' (Welwyn Garden City?).

*Do souls have bones? Ed.

Heav'n-U-Like

Actually, there was quite a good choice of 'better places', as the Aztecs believed in thirteen different heavens. Luckily, there were only nine hells. Babies, who hadn't really had much time to be naughty, went to the 'Heaven of the Milk Tree' (a kid's gotta eat); those who drowned went to the Heaven of Rain (umbrellas not provided) and those that died in battle, childbirth (women mostly), or sacrifice, went to the best heaven of all, which was near the sun.

Blood for All

One of the brilliant things about wars, according to the Aztecs, was that if you won (which most times they did) you'd have literally thousands of prisoners to sacrifice – yippee!

In Inga Clendinnen's *Aztecs* she describes what happened to the losers of the Mexicas' (early Aztecs) battle against the revolting Huaxtecs of the Northern Gulf coast. The triumphant Mexica army dragged their vanquished prisoners all the way back to the capital simply to be killed (what a waste of energy: I'd do 'em on the spot*). The men were linked by a long cord threaded through their noses (see

---

*I bet you would. Ed

Good Ways of Stopping People from Running Away) and the women and children were tied together by heavy wooden collars.

As they approached the city, the priests informed them how fortunate they were to be chosen to be sacrificed at the opening ceremony for their new Temple of Huitzilopochtli (some people have all the luck). Over 20,000 of the poor devils arrived, filling the causeways leading to Tenochtitlan as they waited, rather patiently by all accounts (obviously in no real hurry to be murdered), on their way to the pyramid and eventually the sacrificial stone.

Useless Fact No. 75

One of the reasons that the queue was so docile might well have been due to drugs.

It was quite common to give waiting victims 'obsidian knife-water'. This cheeky little concoction was supposed to be a mixture of the washings from the sacrificial knife mixed with chocolate (mmm! – delicious) and was meant to make everyone jolly cheerful (well, as cheerful as you can be when you're about to have your heart torn out).

But it is more likely to have been the fermented milk of the agave cactus which did the trick. When they got near the top of the steps it is thought that the priests gave them a shot of something stronger still, *ololiuqui* (made from the seeds of the morning glory plant), or *peyotl* (mescalin to you and me*).

Where to Put the Bodies?

Oh dear, *such* a nice few days and all one's left with is headaches, thought the poor Aztecs. What can one do with the 20,000 assorted dead bodies that are left after all the fun? There are only so many of one's fellow men that one can eat at a sitting and meat goes off so quickly in a hot climate, don't you find?

They solved the problem by only eating the arms and legs of their victims, and then thoughtfully throwing the torsos to the rather sensibly-resident birds of prey and the fierce beasts in King Montezuma's menagerie. Skulls, naturally, were put onto spitted skull racks or made into novelty walls (I've heard of walls having ears, but never eyes). The rest of the bits and pieces were presumably burnt on huge fires as there was precious little earth to bury them in.

*It might be known to you, but it certainly isn't known to me. Ed

Glad to be a Gladiator?

If the Aztecs captured a fine warrior in battle they had rather a unique way of disposing of him. They'd save him up (with a few others) for the Festival of the Flaying of Men (sounds jolly, don't you think?), then, one at a time, they'd secure the victim to the centre of a raised, round 'gladiatorial stone' by a rope round his waist. He was kindly given a couple of pints of *pulque* (fermented cactus juice) and some joke weapons — four wooden balls, four flimsy cudgels and a war club — to fight with. The club, instead of having the standard razor-

sharp blades embedded in it, had only feathers (see Very Tame Clubs). He was then required, rather unfairly I think, to fight four massive knights who were equipped with the real things (clubwise).

Of course, these four warriors, who could have brought the poor chap down with one blow (so spoiling the fun) always chose to 'stripe' the guy instead: that is, to cover his body with horrid stripy wounds. When the brave warrior eventually fell, through loss of blood (or boredom), they promptly chopped off his head and pranced around the stone with it. They then removed his skin and his original captor put it on for twenty days. After distributing his arms and legs (four ways, no doubt), they cut out his heart, barbecued it and ate it in a special maize stew (try that on *Junior Masterchef**). Oh well, what d'you expect from gladiators?

Slaves

There are thousands of examples of the beastly things that the Aztecs did to their enemies, but it has to be said that they weren't averse to killing their own slaves and even some of their respected brethren.

There were tons of slaves around, and they came from various sources. Many of them were from far distant lands, taken as payment for a 'won' battle. But there were also slave merchants who would scour the country looking for likely candidates. If a person had fallen into debt through loose

---

*I know you warned us, but this is truly over the top. Ed
Don't blame me! JF

living or gambling, he could, by becoming a slave, wipe out his debt and be looked after by a master. The slight downside to this was being kitted out with a heavy wooden yoke all day and the constant nagging possibility that your name was coming up next on the sacrificial hit list.

> ### Useless Fact No. 78
> It was quite well known for parents to sell off their eldest children to slavery as soon as the younger ones were old enough to do their share of the housework, so just you watch out for your mum and dad talking to tall, dark strangers in low voices.

Bathed Slaves

In order to get your average slave ready for sacrifice, they had to lose their slave status. This was done by a quick sluice-down with the old holy water – so making the subject a 'bathed slave'. But it didn't stop there. They were then trained in dance, speech and deportment (walking proper) which, you must admit, when you think of what it was all for, was a bit like respraying a car before taking it down to the breaker's yard.*

Before the big day the 'ex' slaves were required to sing and dance, bedecked in feathers and flowers at a series of feasts held purely to show off how rich their master was; it was an expensive business buying and training a slave just to be topped. Strangely enough, it appears that the slaves really liked the attention (silly fools) and co-operated all the way. On the day itself, they'd be dressed up to the nines and paraded through the houses of all the boss's rellies before setting off in a procession to the sacrificial pyramid. On the way they'd be attacked and chastised (shouted at and poked

---

*What a daft comparison. Ed

and things like that) by war captives, egged on by their Aztec captors. The only explanation for their complete docility and sometimes even enjoyment of this depressing pantomime, is that by the time they reached the sacrificial stone they were 'stoned' themselves (as explained earlier).

Chapter 8

WHAT A VERY ODD LOT THEY WERE - AZTEC GODS

Aztec gods were famous for being extremely grumpy. The Aztecs thought that if they didn't keep them happy, they'd be in for it big time. Consequently, the poor devils bent over backwards not to offend the gods. Try as they might, however, they always seemed to get it wrong. The trouble was that in that part of the world there were plenty of rather unforeseen circs like earthquakes, droughts, floods and volcanoes, which the Aztecs interpreted as the gods having a go at them.

Priests, etc.
To give you some idea of how important religion was, there were tens of thousands of priests, priestesses, and astrologers (and astrologesses) who were treated to as much forelock-tugging as the noblemen.

Despite all this, a priest's life doesn't sound much of a laugh. As well as having to pray every five minutes and keep the sacred flames alight in the temples, they were expected to give their own blood to the gods, which they collected by pricking various parts of their bodies with sharp thorns.

Mind you, when they got fed up with using their own blood, they turned on others to keep up the supply.

Gods-a-Plenty
There was no shortage of gods for the Aztecs to worship Here are the top five.

Huitzilopochtli
(Left-handed Hummingbird: The God of War and Sun)
One of the Mexicas' (who turned into the Aztecs) very first gods.

He took the form of a sacred 'medical bundle' and was carried around by four 'god bearers'. Huitzilopochtli told them what to do in a high, fast, twittery voice (as all good talking bundles do), and as a prize for leading the Aztecs to fame and fortune he was promoted to 'Warrior God' and 'God of the Sun'.

All the Mexicas' conquests were allowed to keep their own gods, but woe betide them if they didn't worship Huitzilopochtli the most. As for family, his mother was Coaticue, the corpse-eating Earth goddess who'd, rather painfully I should imagine, given birth to the moon and the stars. Huitzilopochtli unfortunately murdered all his brothers and sisters (which is one way of becoming an only child, I suppose).

Useless Fact No. 80
Food and drink-wise, Huitzilopochtli had simple tastes: human hearts washed down with blood.

Tlaloc
 (God of Rain and Fertility)

Easily recognized in the street by his huge, spectacle-shaped mask or his fringe of curved tusks. He was the chap to whom most of the kids and enemies were sacrificed (see Chapters 6 and 7). It was Tlaloc that caused all the trees to grow, the maize to blossom, the grasses to . . . Well, you get the picture. If the Aztecs got up his nose, he sent more water than they'd bargained for, in the form of violent storms, freezing sleet and out-of-season flooding.

Just to illustrate how unreasonable he was, he allowed his personal priests, when coming home from collecting reeds for some big festival or other, to take the possessions of anyone who crossed their path. If they resisted, the priests had permission to beat them 'till the skin came off their bodies'.

That's priests for you!

Quetzalcoatl
(God of Priestly Wisdom and Nature)

This one created mankind in rather a novel way.

One day, as he was strolling through the domains of the Lord of the Dead (as you do), he began gathering up the bones of dead men and women from old, extinct civilizations (taking care to keep them separate). Unfortunately, while running away from the somewhat miffed Death Lord, he tripped and dropped the bones, which promptly shattered. He picked up all the bits, shoved them all in a carrier bag (he presumably could no longer tell which were girl bones and which were boy bones) and took them to a lady god called Cihuacoatl (Woman Snake) who ground them into a fine bisexual meal. Then Quetzalcoatl and his god mates drew blood from their private parts (ouch!) to moisten the ground-up bones so making a dough (presumably pink). A man and a woman were then modelled from this dough.

C'mon, it's no more daft than Eve being made out of Adam's rib, etc.

Useless and Very Dubious Fact No. 84

Though Quetzalcoatl was happy to be a bloke during the day, he turned himself into a dog-headed monster called Fido – sorry – Xolotl in the evenings.

At least he could take himself for walkies.

Tezcatlipoca

(Lord of the Here and Now)

Together with Quetzalcoatl, he seized the limbs of the Great Earth Monster as she swam the primeval waters, and rather rudely tore her in half, thus forming the earth and sky.

A very busy god this one, and a bit of a Jekyll-and-Hyde to boot.

His main duties were to supply kids to their mummies and daddies, decide what and who they should look like and determine how well they would do in their lives. In addition, if a rich and powerful man suddenly lost the lot (or the plot), it was down to Tezcatlipoca. Likewise if a poor man suddenly got lucky, it was also down to 'The Capricious Creator'. The poor old Aztecs didn't dare make him *too* happy either because, if he laughed, it meant a bout of death and destruction – which was certainly no joke.

On his special festival, all the slaves were given the day off. Their wooden collars were removed and everyone had to make a fuss of them.

Anyone who gave them a hard time was 'visited with pustulating sores and killed on the killing stone'. Next day, of course, they could treat the poor so-and-sos just as before (with an extra kick for good measure).

Xipe Totec
(The Flayed Lord: God of Fertility, Springtime and Vegetables – sorry – Vegetation)
Funny old god this one. For a start he painted his head red with yellow stripes (don't try this at home). Xipe got his kicks by ordering that his sacrificial victims be flayed (skinned alive). After this his priests would put on the bloody skin, decorated by

quail feathers, and dance around quite happily until they 'stank like dead dogs'.

Weird or what? For some reason this symbolized the springtime renewal of vegetation. Work that one out.

Useless Fact No. 89
There were so many little local godlets throughout the Aztec lands that the peasants had to call them by a group name . . . The Four Hundred Rabbits.*

*Why? Ed
Don't ask me. JF

Chapter 9

THOSE DRATTED SPANISH!
or...
ALL GOOD THINGS COME TO AN END

The Aztec civilization had been running along just fine – better than fine, in fact – but in 1518 things started to go a *bit* wrong before the whole business went *properly* wrong.

First of all there was a string of natural disasters; horrendous hurricanes, frightful floods, furious fires and even an outbreak of deformed kids. None of the wise men, soothsayers (what *is* a sooth, and how do you say it?) or magicians had a clue as to what it was all about, but their boss Montezuma II, known for being a bit of a misery anyway, reckoned it was the first knockings of something much more catastrophic to come. Oh boy, did he get that right.

Seen at the Seaside
Reports came back to Montezuma in 1519 of eleven huge, floating towers populated by six hundred deathly-white

men (civil servants?) with long beards (never seen before) arriving on the Pacific coast. They commanded monstrous machines that spat fire and tossed out huge round balls of stone.

Most terrifying of all, however, were the glinting metal men (covered from head to foot in armour) who seemed to be in charge of huge, black, hairless sorts of llamas (horses) that allowed them to ride on their backs and go wherever they told them.

Being simple, superstitious folk, the Aztecs jumped to the only conclusion possible – these guys were gods. And what do you do to gods? Worship them, of course.

Time for Presents

Montezuma sent messengers to meet the new arrivals with fabulous gifts: the ceremonial jewellery and clothes of the god Quetzalcoatl; a huge, cartwheel-sized disk of pure gold and an even bigger silver one; their most treasured feathered head-dresses and a whole assortment of other precious Aztec knick-knacks. But it must be said that the Spaniards were only really interested in gold, gold and more gold, which they fell upon 'like monkeys – lusting for it like pigs';

they simply ignored all the other stuff. The 'visiting' Spaniards weren't daft, however: in return for all this fab treasure they gave the Aztecs – wait for it – three shirts and a cup. I don't know about you, but if I'd have been an Aztec, I'd have felt a little cheated. Anyway, they didn't even wear shirts.

Useless Fact No. 99

Montezuma also sent copious amounts of food and drink to Cortez (the Spaniards' boss) and his merry men/gods but, as his messengers left to meet the visitors, Montezuma threw in a chilling suggestion.

> *'If, by any chance, he does not like the food that you give him, and is desirous of devouring human beings and wishes to eat you, allow yourselves to be eaten.'*

I think I might just have forgotten that suggestion on the way.

Wild Goose Chase

Montezuma wasn't daft, but despite his efforts to keep the conquistadors from his capital Tenochtitlan (which included sending them on a route that went over a cliff), the Spaniards finally pitched up at the super city, having bolstered their forces with all the Native American tribes that they'd defeated on the way.

The poor locals had soon realized that the newcomers didn't fight proper. Cortez's guys tortured and killed the representatives who'd arrived, cap-in-hand, at their camp, and wiped out whole villages as they crossed their path, murdering all the unarmed men, women, children and pets. The tricksy Spaniards even used their crossbows and cannons to kill from a distance, instead of fighting hand to hand like decent warriors (that's modern technology for you). Worst of all, they just killed the ones they didn't want as Aztec battle fodder, instead of capturing them for later sacrifice (though it wouldn't make much difference to me if I was the victim!).

Basically, the whole way they did battle simply wasn't cricket.

Useless Fact No. 100
It turned out that, early on, the Aztecs were more terrified of the horses than the men – all that stamping, snorting and rearing onto their hind legs really freaked them out (and that was just the soldiers!).

Into the City
The Spaniards eventually marched straight into Tenochtitlan, having kidded the Aztecs that they wanted to pay tribute to their ruler, but the cheeky monkeys immediately took poor Montezuma hostage – it really wasn't his year.

When head-Spaniard Cortez decided to take a little break to fight off a rival Spanish army, the inhabitants of the city, finally seeing the invaders for the ungodlike creatures they really were, rose up and murdered half of 'em, driving the rest from the city. Sadly, Montezuma was killed in all the fuss, but his subjects had lost respect for him anyway, so that was OK.

Oh No! They're Back
You can't keep a good – sorry – bad Spaniard down. Within a year Cortez and a much bigger army were back and, with the help of the turncoat lakeside communities, put the whole island under siege by just blocking off the causeways. Cortez then built twelve brigantines (two-masted fighting ships) whose cannons bombarded the city while keeping the lake free of those pesky Aztec canoes. The Spaniards then cut off the water and prevented any food from reaching Tenochtitlan.

The siege lasted four months and during that time 240,000 people died from starvation (and probably a bit from thirst). They had resorted to eating anything right down to lizards, weeds and slime from the lake, Egg McMuffins* and even old bits of leather. By the end of the siege the streets were piled with unburied, half-eaten corpses, which the Spaniards (while clutching their noses) had to step over when they finally stormed into Tenochtitlan.

No Prize for Cortez

Poor old Cortez had thought that he could present his king back home with a magnificent shiny city, but when he looked around, after such a ferocious battle/siege, fought over such a long period of time, his prize was no more than a mass of

*I rather like Egg McMuffins. Ed

stinking, bloodstained rubble. The Spaniards, true to form, ordered that all the priests be set upon and ripped apart by their biggest and fiercest dogs, and that the prettier women and boys be savagely branded on their faces and set to work as slaves. The menfolk were forced to build a new city for their new masters. Even the poor long-suffering and probably well-miffed gods were given their marching orders. The mighty Aztec civilization was well and truly trashed. Shame really!

Chapter 10

NEW SPAIN

So what happened to one of the most powerful and exciting cultures in history? Surely its light couldn't just set in the west without any more trace or significance than yesterday's sun (or should that be *Sun*?). The Spanish, as you might know, were, and still very much are, Catholics, and one of their motives for conquest was to convert the 'heathen' Aztecs to their way of thinking. Well, that's what they'd have liked the rest of the world to think. Everyone knows that the real reason for going to all that trouble was to squeeze as much gold out of the poor heathens as possible. Cortez, who by this time was living like a god himself, went to terrifying lengths, like burning the feet of Cuauhtemoc, Montezuma's successor, to find where all their treasure was hidden.*

Not a Happy Spain

Strangely enough, back home in Spain, the powers that be were becoming a trifle concerned at the lurid reports of what their bully-boy conquistadors were up to. It's one thing building up your gold reserves and setting out to create what they called, rather originally, New Spain, but maybe annihilating an entire civilization could be regarded as slightly extreme.

Feeling guilty, the Spanish passed loads of laws to try to make things better, but Cortez and his boys paid scant

---

*Why? Was he standing on it? Ed
Don't ask me. JF

attention. They really were too far away for their home-based bosses to do them any real harm, and anyway as long as they kept sending the loot home, they knew they'd eventually turn a blind eye to how they'd gone about getting it. Eventually, however, in 1535, Cortez was replaced by Don Antonio de Mendoza, Spain's first Viceroy.

They chose to build the City of Mexico (now called – you've guessed – Mexico City) on the pile of old rubble that had once been Tenochtitlan. To be perfectly honest, the poorer peasants noticed very little difference between the new rulers and the old. If you are used to being treated like garbage, I suppose it doesn't matter too much who's doing it to you. If you've spent your life slaving from dawn to dusk building pyramids, what's the big deal about switching to churches? The main plus was

that, unlike under their old masters, they were able to drink whenever they liked*. The poor Spaniards found drunkenness amongst the workforce a terrible problem.

They were even able to hang on to some of their leaders – but they were leaders in word only, because they all had to answer to the Spanish boss of the time. It was just an easy way for keeping the natives in some sort of order so that they could squeeze more 'tribute' out of them. Tribute was the price the poor residents had to pay in either cash, goods or labour, for being 'protected' by their new masters. Great – there they were, virtual slaves, and having to pay for the privilege as well. Not altogether fair, methinks.

Dirty Devils
The whole thing eventually proved to be a living hell for the workers. Not only did they end up in forced labour camps, watching everything they produced going straight to their new masters, but there was a much, much bigger threat – disease.

*Don't you mean 'the main *difference*'? Ed

The Spanish brought with them a whole new bunch of foreign viruses, like influenza, that the ex-Aztecs had no defences against. It wiped out such a huge percentage of the population that Mexico never really recovered until this century. For ages it was one of the most sparsely populated countries in the world.

Idol Moments
On the religious front, things were a little smoother. The natives actually quite liked the first Franciscan monks that came over because, for the first time ever, someone seemed more than a little concerned with their plight. In fact, they liked the monks so much that they actually helped to destroy 500 of their own temples and 20,000 of their best idols and sacred *codices* (storybooks).

Only a handful of years after they'd seen the Spanish appear on the horizon, nearly all traces of the Aztecs' ancient and majestic way of life had disappeared. I bet that taught them not to talk to strangers . . .

TIME'S UP

Well, I don't know about you, but given the choice of being an Aztec or staying as I am, I think I'd choose the latter. As you must have realized, I've only given you the briefest outline of what those strange people were all about, but then, what else could you get for just a couple of quid that would keep you busy, intrigued, educated and amused for a couple of hours (actually, please don't answer that).

If you do want to know more, there should be a few 'proper' books on Aztecs in your local library. They will contain tons more information than mine,* but I bet they won't be as much fun and, anyway, you won't be able to get into (or out of) anything else nearly as quickly. Talking of anything else, why not try some of the other subjects in this magnificent and mind-expanding series what I have written. Having said that, I beg of you, please don't read 'em quicker than I can write 'em.

*Not difficult. Ed